A PSYCHOLOGICAL STUDY
OF
IMMIGRANT CHILDREN
AT
ELLIS ISLAND

BY

BERTHA M. BOODY

A DISSERTATION SUBMITTED TO THE BOARD OF UNIVERSITY
STUDIES OF THE JOHNS HOPKINS UNIVERSITY IN CONFORMITY
WITH THE REQUIREMENTS FOR THE DEGREE OF
DOCTOR OF PHILOSOPHY

MENTAL MEASUREMENT MONOGRAPHS

Published by THE WILLIAMS & WILKINS COMPANY

| Serial No. 3 | BALTIMORE, MD. | February, 1926 |

A PSYCHOLOGICAL STUDY OF IMMIGRANT CHILDREN AT ELLIS ISLAND[1]

BERTHA M. BOODY

[1] Chapters III and IV only are presented here. The complete study was published as *Mental Measurement Monographs*, Serial No. 3.

CHAPTER III

REVIEW OF LAWS AT THE TIME OF THIS STUDY AND OF CERTAIN REPORTS BEARING UPON THEM

At this point, in order to have in mind more fully, the place at which the country was in the gradual development of its immigration system at the beginning of this study it is perhaps necessary to make a short survey of the progress of the law, especially as it concerns the mental side of the immigrant.

Only after 1820 was any definite count made,[1] and the date of the first legislation by the national government, in regard to immigration did not come till 1882.[2] Before this time, both regulation and inspection, had rested entirely with the individual states,[3] although the inadequacy of the plan was increasingly felt. Even after 1882, complete federal control was not established for nearly another decade.

It is hard to realize that up till so late a date, the actual responsibility in regard to immigration, had not been a matter of national care, and it is perhaps equally a cause for wonder that in the forty odd years in which the government has assumed control, so much[4] has been done.

That the mental make up of the immigrant early called for attention, is no surprise. The strictness[5] of the law in this respect has steadily increased. Below are listed the various kinds of mental defect, in their classes, followed by the date at which they appeared upon the excluded list.

Lunatics (insane)	1882[6]
Idiots	1882
Epileptics	1903
Imbeciles	1907[7]
Feebleminded	1907
Mentally or physically defective	1907
(Such defect as may affect the ability to earn a living)	
Constitutional Psychopathic Inferiority	1917[8,9]

In 1915 for the first time, the "Mentally or Physically Defective" class, was separated into "Mentally Defective" on the one

22

side and "Physically Defective" on the other, so that from this date on, we find the two separate classifications.

Another change of interest—that has been found necessary at two separate times—is in regard to the "Insane." In 1903 instead of the simple earlier reading, the law was made to read,[10] as follows: "Insane" and "persons who have been insane within five years previous, and also "persons who have had two or more attacks of insanity at any time previously." In 1917 there was further change and the clause was worded "Insane" and "Persons who have had one or more attacks of insanity at any time previously." These varying phrases suggest the difficulty that has been found in the interpretation of "Insane."

Other points in the general development that should be noted are:

1. The steady increase of the Federal Head Tax. In 1882 we find it $.50; in the text[11] of the Law of 1917, it stands at $8, children however under sixteen who accompany their father and mother not being subject to the tax. People in discussing the immigration question often forget that this source of revenue for expenses exists.

2. That the deportation of aliens admitted[12] contrary to law, at first (in 1891) only possible within one year after landing, then within two years and then three years, is by the Law of 1917, allowed at any time within five years after entrance into the country. Anarchists, and persons who were criminals before coming to the United States may be deported, however, "irrespective of the time of their entry," and since 1910 the same has been true for prostitutes and those connected with prostitution.

This deportation after entrance is another fact that is sometimes almost forgotten, but if one has once seen, for instance, a group of 150, collected from different parts of the country, and brought to Ellis Island to be put on ships from there, it is not forgotten.[13]

3. That in 1907, the law required steamship[14] companies to furnish lists of outgoing passengers. This seems important in the consideration of the whole question of immigration. Who goes back, may be as important as who stays.

4. That the fines for bringing in aliens[15] not admitted by law were both increased, in 1917 over the Law of 1907, and extended

as well, to further classes, while an added penalty is imposed in that the steamship company so fined must pay also an amount equal to that paid by each alien for his transportation, this amount to be turned over to the debarred alien by a United States official.[16]

5. That an appeal to a Medical Board of Officers of the United States Public Health Service is allowed in mental cases, where the alien, if he so chooses, may introduce one expert medical witness—another step made in 1917.[17]

6. That before the "Boards of Special Inquiry" into doubtful cases, aliens may have witnesses.

These points, singled out from many, are specially emphasized; because remembrance of them is many times a great help, to understanding.

We now have come to the consideration of a provision which in spite of much criticism, is probably more far reaching in its beneficial effect on the mental well being of the country than anything before it, however important, has been, with the exception of the exclusion of the feebleminded in 1907. This is the establishing in 1917, of the so-called "Illiteracy Test."[18]

For twenty years the question of some sort of "reading test" had appeared at intervals in the deliberations of Congress. In 1897 President Cleveland vetoed a general immigration bill largely because it contained such a clause. In 1898 a bill of like nature passed the Senate; but was lost in the House; yet still the question persisted. Two other Presidents gave their veto, President Taft and President Wilson, who even vetoed twice. But over this last veto Congress finally passed the measure.

The "Immigration Commission" created by Congress, had in its report spoken of some such provision as "the most feasible single means" of bringing[19] about desired restriction. The amount of effect that such a test would have, was of course unknown. What it might be, could only be conjectured, as no existing figures covered the problem as it stood. We must now look a bit at the law and its working.

By its provisions, in addition to the classes already excluded by law, the following are excluded: "All aliens over 16, physically capable of reading, who can not read the English language, or some other language or dialect including Hebrew and Yiddish."

Then come the exceptions, and as it all bears so closely on this study, they may be quoted in detail. The wording goes on: "Provided: That any admissible alien, or any alien heretofore or hereafter legally admitted, or any citizen of the United States, may bring in or send for his father or grandfather over fifty-five years of age, his wife, his mother, his grandmother, or his unmarried or widowed daughter, if otherwise admissible whether such relative can read or not, and such relative shall be permitted to enter." The law provides definite instructions for its own carrying out. The immigrant inspector is to provide slips of uniform size prepared under the direction of the Secretary of Labor, "each containing not less than 30 nor more than 40 words in ordinary use, printed in plainly legible type in some one of the various languages or dialects of immigrants." Each alien is to designate his particular language, and is required to read the words printed on the slip in such language.

Then follow in the law the exempt classes (individuals fleeing from religious persecution, people in transit, etc.) always a most interesting as well as dangerous section, but not of special moment perhaps in our present consideration. Commissioner Husband, in discussing[20] the law, points out that this test is qualitative and not quantitative; for if the illiterate are excluded, the literate may come in their places, so that numbers may not be affected.

He also points out that the test is simple, and that "anyone could fit himself to meet it in a short time if he so desired." This seems to me in a way true, and in a way not. In any case, I should say that the facts as they stand are not in the least detrimental to the value of the test. If the test can be prepared for, then surely anyone capable of such preparation[21] is not of the kind that the law meant to exclude.

Although we cannot in any way compare the "illiteracy" figures of 1914, with any results obtained under the working of the 1917 law, as the old figures by "illiteracy" meant lack of both reading and writing, and had 14 years as the age limit, yet I do want to show from a racial interest, the worst nationalities there quoted in this regard.

	per cent illiterate
Turkish	62.6[22]
Portuguese	49.5

Dalmatian, Bosnian, Herzeggovinian.................. 45.9
Syrian.. 43.8
Lithuanian... 41.7
Italian: South... 41.2

The law went into effect May 5, 1917. Within the first two months, 391 illiterates were excluded,[23] and the Commissioner General, even after that short trial, was willing to say that the new law was in most, if not all respects, "an eminently satisfactory piece of legislation, that would be of great benefit to the country." The series of slips[24] prepared for use in the test, are of two kinds; one, the sentences to be used where it is possible to have an interpreter through whom the reading may be done, the other a standard set of directions in the various languages, the carrying out of which will show the inspector whether or not the alien has been able to read.

At Ellis Island, the first kind is seen in operation, and it seems in a way the better one of the two as a "literacy test," since the second kind includes in its performance more than the fact of literacy. The second is of course, in any case, only necessary where interpreters are not present.

In watching the ease and the speed with which this test is handled, one wonders if this same simple and easily running means might not be used by some slight extension, so that it would indicate certain further mental facts. In the handling of the test much reasonableness and kindness[25] are displayed, at the same time with exactness and care.

To show "the efficacy of the illiteracy test as a preventive measure" the following figures, as given in the Immigration Report of 1920, are set down.[26]

Illiterate aliens admitted, 1908–1917, inclusive, fourteen years of age and over

1908........... 172,293 (total admissions,   782,870)[27]
1909........... 191,049 (total admissions,   751,786)
1910.... .... 253,569 (total admissions, 1,041,570)
1911........ ... 182,273 (total admissions,   878,587)
1912........... 177,284 (total admissions,   838,172)
1913........... 269,988 (total admissions, 1,197,892)
1914........... 260,152 (total admissions, 1,218,480)
1915........... 35,067 (total admissions,   326,700)⎫
1916........... 40,138 (total admissions,   298,826)⎬ war years
1917...(to May 5) 35,215 (total admissions,   295,403)⎭
    Total...... 1,617,018

The larger proportion of these illiterates could have been excluded, the Commissioner General says, had the literacy bill been in effect. He reminds us too, that its effect is measured not only by the number of those who attempt to enter in spite of it, and are rejected, but to a much greater degree by the number who are deterred from starting.

For 1918 and 1919 the "illiterates" who were admitted (according to the Law of 1917, i.e. those who cannot read) show the following figures:

1918..................... 3772 (total admissions, 110,618)[28]
1919..................... 2827 (total admissions, 141,132)

In 1920, 1921, 1922 and 1923 the result is shown in the accompanying table. The figures must be interpreted in the light of the fact that the 3 per cent law (to be spoken of later),[29] was in effect for 28 days in 1921, was operative of course not at all, in 1920, and was in use through the entire years of 1922 and 1923.[30]

Illiterate aliens admitted

	MALE	FEEBLE	TOTAL	REASONS FOR ADMISSION	TOTAL ADMISSIONS PER YEAR
1920	2,190	12,904	15,094	14,741 join relatives 9 religious persecution 343 other causes 1 physically defective	430,001
1921	3,287	24,176	27,463	27,338 join relatives 120 other causes 4 religious persecution 1 physically defective	805,228
1922 (3 per cent law)	1,476	9,267	10,743	10,680 join relatives 55 other causes 7 religious persecution 1 physically defective	309,556
1923 (3 per cent law)	2,001	9,355	11,356	11,304 join relatives 52 other causes	522,919

The per cent of "illiterates" to the total number of immigrants admitted, therefore, runs about as follows:

```
                                           per cent
1908.................................... 22 (14 years)
1909.................................... 25
1910.................................... 24
1911.................................... 20
1912.................................... 21
1913.................................... 22
1914.................................... 21
1915.................................... 10⎫
1916.................................... 13⎬ war years
1917.................................... 11⎭
10 years (1908–1917).................... 21
1918.................................... 3 (16 years)
1919.................................... 2
1920.................................... 3
1921.................................... 3
1922.................................... 3
1923.................................... 2
```

Although, as we have said, it is not safe to draw conclusions on figures so difficultly based, still one perhaps may feel somewhat encouraged by them as to the mental status of the country.

Two things here seem to call for special notice. One is to mark how far among the admissions, the illiteracy of women exceeds that of men, a very anxious state of affairs for the family life in new surroundings. The second point, is in regard to race— to see, for 1922 and 1923 what European races, in the number of their illiterates admitted, now lead the list. The actual figures are set down here, as well as the per cent, for although the per cent bears particularly on the standing of the race, as represented in our immigration, still for another side, the numbers themselves, are the most important.

The two highest are:

	NUMBER ADMITTED	ILLITERATES	PER CENT
For 1922:			
Hebrew........................	53,524	3,884	7
South Italian.................	35,056	2,820	8
For 1923:			
South Italian.................	39,266	2,721	6.9
Hebrew........................	49,719	2,496	5

The study of the working results of this test, is a very important thing. After some years of trial, it was referred to before the House Committee on Immigration as follows:[31] "In the opinion of the Government Officials and expert students of the matter, the reading test has proved to be one of the most valuable features of the law."

Before leaving the question, it may be of interest to set down a few figures as to the European races debarred by the test during the fiscal years 1922 and 1923.[32]

RACE	ADMITTED (TOTAL)		DEBARRED FOR ILLITERACY	
	1922	1923	1922	1923
French......................	13,617	34,371	284	672
Italian, South...	35,056	39,226	133	118
Hebrew......................	53,524	49,719	55	93
English......................	30,429	60,524	43	95
Irish......................	17,191	30,386	31	76
Polish.............	6,357	13,210	28	57
German......................	31,218	65,543	14	41

Only those European races are given where the number debarred is higher than twenty a year, with the exception of the German figure in 1922 which stands at 14. The fairly consistent positions held by the races as far as actual numbers debarred are concerned, is of interest, as is also the strangely high figure for the French in both years.

The total numbers debarred from all races for illiteracy as compared with total admissions for 1922 and 1923 stand as follows:

	TOTAL ADMISSIONS	DEBARRED FOR ILLITERACY
1922	309,556	1,249
1923	522,919	2,095

To close this survey a brief table is given of those European races which, in largest numbers, are deported after entry, for illiteracy reasons:

	1922	1923[33]
English................................	13	No separate listing made
French...................................	25	
Italian (South)......	19	
Spanish..................................	20	

These are the races showing above 10, and it will be seen that they include all those in the debarred table, with the exception of Hebrews and Poles. Of the Poles only 6 were deported after entrance, and of the Hebrews but 3. The total number in 1922 deported after entrance, in this regard, stands at 274.

Next for consideration must come the so-called 3 per cent law, to which reference has already been made.[34] By the provisions of this law, 3 per cent of the number of any given nationality here in the country according to the census of 1910, might be admitted each year as the quota for the said nation, the country of birth determining nationality.

This is the Act of May 19, 1921, which went into effect at midnight June 2, 1921, to be operative until the end of the fiscal year of 1922—that is till June 30. To give time for further study into the almost limitless details of the entire question, Congress by the joint resolution of May 11, 1922, extended the law for two years, from June 30, 1922, to June 30, 1924.

According to the law not more than 20 per cent of the annual quota of a nationality might be admitted in any month, said quota to be determined by the Secretary of State, the Secretary of Commerce, and the Secretary of Labor in joint conference.[35]

It has been for some time fairly clear that some sort of restriction to immigration has the backing of public opinion, but it is also true, that apart from those who wish unrestricted immigration, for labor or racial reasons there do exist people who believe that the movement of men, should, by the rights of the case, be free.

Commissioner General Husband,[36] in his review of this law, after a year's trial, pointed out the fact, that in comparison with

309,556 admissions, there were 13,731 rejections, a decrease of but 48 from the rejections of the previous year, when the entering number was three times as large, thus seeming to suggest, that with the smaller numbers to be handled, greater efficiency in detecting defects, could be counted upon. In his discussion he refers to six other important things to be noted in the working of the law. I shall refer to four of these which must be kept in mind for a clear understanding of certain processes at Ellis Island.

1. The law does not apply to certain classes:

> Government officials and their families, etc.
> Aliens in transit
> Tourists or temporary visitors
> Aliens under eighteen, who are children of United States citizens.

In special inquiry cases, traces of a knowledge of this section were often found—sometimes, however, too late. The classification had to be a bona fide one.

2. The following classes are counted against a quota so long as the quota exists; but may be admitted after such quota is exhausted:

> Aliens returning from a temporary visit abroad
> Aliens who are professors, actors, etc.

This again is a clause that demanded in its application—and got—a very close scrutiny.

3. Preference is to be given to certain specified persons, in so far as possible (wives, parents, etc.). The discussion of this section on the floor of Congress left no doubt as to the belief in the universal existence of human relationships.

4. That the Commissioner General is to publish each month a statement showing the status of the quotas of the various nationalities, which statement shall be issued weekly after 75 per cent of the annual quota of any nationality is exhausted.

Mr. Husband's conclusion as to the working of this law in actual operation ran as follows:

> The administration of the quota law during its initial year, developed many problems, and especially during the first six months of its operation, greatly overtaxed the machinery of the service, and particularly the

facilities at Ellis Island; but now that it is possible to review its accomplishments, unaffected by its discouragements, I do not hesitate to say, that the per centum limit law has accomplished the purpose for which it was obviously enacted, with a degree of success which few anticipated.

The law came naturally under a tremendous fire of criticism. Its weak spots were seen, by no one better probably than by those in charge of its enforcement. This statement therefore is of interest.

As to what the new Immigration regulations should be, the law to supersede this 3 per cent law at the time of its expiration on June 30, 1924, there was much debate. House Resolution 14273[37] introduced in the House of Representatives on February 9, 1923, and referred to the Committee on Immigration and Naturalization,[38] shows the general trend which suggestion for the new legislation took. There is set up a 2 per cent limitation, based on the census of 1890 with a "400 in addition" proviso. To guard against the overcrowding of the first few months of the year, which the wording of the 3 per cent present law had caused, not more than 10 per cent of the permitted immigration was to come in from any country in a given month, leaving, of course, where a quota was small, certain discretionary steps to the Commissioner, with the approval of the Secretary of Labor.

Other suggestions, were an increase in the per cent instead of a decrease, or a quota basis not of numbers of a nationality in the country; but of numbers naturalized. In commenting on this last idea, Commissioner Husband[39] said that Southern European peoples had seldom been more than 50 per cent naturalized, while a much larger percentage of the North and West of Europe, had become citizens.

Certain figures have been quoted[40] in this regard (according to the 1910 census):

Foreign born males of voting age naturalized (1910 census)

Northern and Western Europe:

	per cent
Germany	69.5
Wales	69.2
Ireland	67.8
Sweden	62.8

```
Switzerland..........................................  61.8
Denmark.............................................  61.6
Norway..............................................  57.1
Netherlands.........................................  56.8
France..............................................  49.6
Belgium ............................................  43.0
```

Eastern and Southern Europe:

```
Turkey in Europe....................................  43.0
Rumania.............................................  28.8
Russia..............................................  26.1
Portugal............................................  24.9
Austria.............................................  24 6
Turkey in Asia......................................  21.2
Italy...............................................  17.7
Spain...............................................  16.4
Hungary.............................................  14.3
Greece..............................................   6.6
```

These tables are particularly interesting in one thing which they do not say. As one watches the lines passing before the Immigration Inspectors, and listens to the answers to the question as to prospective citizenship, one thing that stands out always, seems to be the non-committal answers, or the "No's" of the English. In this quoted table of the "North and West," they do not appear.

For some reasons this basis would seem a bad one on which to build a quota determination. The pressure that would in all probability be brought to bear, would not, we may surmise tend to heighten the idea of citizenship.

There are two other lines of thought which were often spoken of by the Secretary of Labor:[41] One is the "selection of immigrants by examination before departure from the Old World, involving the exclusion of undesirables and the admission only of immigrants able to pass just tests of physical and mental health." The second is the enrollment here of aliens admitted, and a census of aliens over a period of years, by the Naturalization Bureau.

The first of the two points, that of examination abroad, is one which has constantly been mentioned, but mentioned generally without going into any of the reasons why so obvious a proceeding had not been adopted. Two or three quotations may show what some of the difficulties have been. The first comes from a speaker quoted in the Congressional Record.[42]   "With reference to foreign inspection and the attitude of foreign governments toward our sifting out the undesirables on their soil, my understanding is that some years ago, the State Department canvassed the situation and many foreign governments objected."

Jenks and Lauck in referring to the question say:[43]

It has frequently been suggested that some system should be devised by which immigrants may be inspected before leaving their homes for a port of embarkation. Such an arrangement, would of course, prevent many hardships now suffered by the thousands that are annually turned back . . . . but this is a subject over which our government has no supervision, the governments of the home countries being the only ones which could take effective action.

Mr. Ashman Brown, in the *Seattle Times*,[44] after mentioning the possibility of selection at the source, said that the plan "is quite in accord with what the President had in mind; but that protests have already come from Greece and Italy, which say that they cannot agree to have the United States setting up the machinery of its government within their borders."

. Secretary Davis, who has spoken most strongly on the hardships of examination on this side of the ocean, said only this in regard to examination on a foreign shore: that he has informed the President that the Department's Solicitor is now going into the matter.[45]

The Public Health Service does have representatives at certain foreign ports who act "merely in an advisory capacity," as reports are most careful to state. It is perhaps interesting to note the wording:

The function, however, of medical[46] officers stationed in foreign ports is not to reject aliens found suffering from any of the mental or physical diseases, deportable under the "Immigration" laws of the United States; but merely to notify the proper authorities in the ports, that immigrants suffering from these diseases are liable to be deported upon their arrival in the United States.

Or we may find the statement in regard to the position of these officials more explicit still:[47]

This procedure does not contemplate the issuance of a certificate, nor does it prevent the embarkation of the alien examined, even though he is found to be defective. It affords opportunity, however, for information from the medical examiner to the intending immigrant, and to the steamship agent as to any defect.

Each Public Health Service report makes this advisory aspect clear in a briefer or longer phrase.

From a United States point of view, also objections have existed to examinations in Europe.[48] Such examination could never do away wholly with examination on this side of the ocean, because of epidemic danger, and certain other conditions that might develop[49] during the long voyage. "Counting" on the other side is of course a possibility; but final medical decision probably must be determined by the alien's condition at the actual time of entry. Then too the wide distribution of the ports of departure would offer questions not found, where as we have seen, one large port of entry deals with such a very large percentage of all the arrivals.

Under the present system there are of course great hardships; but experience at Ellis Island makes one not so much wonder at the hardships, as stand amazed at the chances people are willing to take.

In all this looking foward to future methods for the determining of the best kind of immigration, "numbers" though necessarily more or less to the fore, did not overshadow "kind." Commissioner Husband even said: "Numbers do not matter so much. I think[50] that Congress would be willing to let in a million immigrants a year, if the country needed them, provided they were of the material best fitted to become United States citizens."[51]

And on the question of kind, Congressional Committees were gathering information. An interesting resolution[52] which was referred by the House of Representatives to the Committee on Immigration, called on the Secretary of Labor and the Surgeon General to show why some such scheme of mental testing as that which had proved successful in the army, should not be employed at Immigration Stations. The Psychological Corporation in New York City, to which a copy of this resolution was sent by the Chairman of the Committee, with a request for comment, sent out to various psychologists throughout the country, letters asking for suggestions in the matter, so that a tabulated report of the answers might be put in the Chairman's hands.

The biologists too were called upon. This report is so closely bound up with a psychological study of the question, that it may be of help to look at it. It was submitted to the Committee on Immigration and Naturalization of the House of Representatives in the 67th Congress, by Dr. H. H. Laughlin,[53] of the Eugenics Record Office of the Carnegie Institution of Washington. The report is from the point of view of genetics, and is based on figures obtained by sending blanks, as to inmates of alien stock, to all state and national "custodial" institutions. The study is one of "bad" elements therefore, to be followed, it is announced by a study of the "good."

Out of 677 institutions to which blanks were sent, 445 cooperated. The results are obtained from birth and parentage records. The classes which Dr. Laughlin uses are nine:

Insanity
Crime
Feeblemindedness
Dependent
Tuberculosis
Epilepsy
Deafness
Blindness
Deformity

These are not the listings of the immigration law, though all, of course, are included in its measures, the law, having somewhat more than 30 distinct classes.[54]

Dr. Laughlin after referring to the points of numbers, and nations, in immigration control, says that the third factor in such control, has to do with the "individual physical, mental and moral quality,"[55] and more particularly with "the potentiality of the immigrant as a parent of desirable Americans of the future." The analysis of this "third factor," is the subject of his investigation. Speaking more specifically, the study is "a measure of the relative soundness of recent and older immigrant stocks."

"Percentages" or "quotas" were determined for each specific

class of defect, for each nationality, on the assumption that the figures for each nation in regard to this defect should bear to the figures for the same defect throughout the entire population, the same relation that the general population figures of the given race, held to the figures of the total population of the United States. That is, if a nation "furnishes inmates of these institutions[56] in the same proportion as it furnishes inhabitants to the United States" it fulfills its quota by 100 per cent. "These percentages of quota[57] fulfillment are the yard-sticks for comparing different groups." The first part of the study deals with immigrants themselves, the second part deals with descendents of immigrants, that is, with the second generation.

The study has seven most interesting charts; but the fact that actual numbers are not given, closely attached to the "per cents" in which these tables are expressed, may lead an observer to notions that are eminently wrong.

For instance Serbia's prominent place[58] at the end of the chart for feeblemindedness, with its long black line reaching out to 220 per cent, does not at all correspond to what you find for Serbia when you turn to the tables for feeblemindedness further on. There you find, as to numbers, that the quota fulfillment allowed one individual. The number found was two. Certainly where the cases are so few, such tables show nothing, and really mislead, when taken apart from actual numbers.

Other information which seems necessary here, particularly when the cases are few, is as to family. It might be quite possible if 200 per cent represents two people, that we are dealing with one socially inadequate family, which could hardly come under a heading of nationality. After watching certain families passing through Ellis Island, one might think it possible to say a higher "per cent" still, and have this statement stay true.

In this whole question, it seems that "actual numbers" are so important, that to consider per cents without them is not in any way a safe procedure. Dr. Laughlin has the actual numbers, in great detail, in tables at the back of his pamphlet, covering the last sixty pages. The three sections which have particularly to do with mental defect—insanity, feeblemindedness and epilepsy—are, of course, the ones which bear especially on this study.

With regard to insanity. All European groups go over their allotment in varying degrees, with the exception of three:

COUNTRY	NUMBER OF INSANE FOUND	QUOTA FULFILLMENT
		per cent
Wales.................................	62	87.50
Switzerland............................	81	69.23
Montenegro............................	3	60 0

The three highest records run as follows:

COUNTRY	NUMBER OF INSANE FOUND	QUOTA FULFILLMENT
		per cent
Ireland.............................	3,782	305 44
Russia, Finland........................	4,212	265 95
Scandinavia...........................	2,203	193 33

This leaves out of consideration certain countries which may have a high per cent, but where the cases are less than 100. For Northwestern Europe the per cent is given as 198.36. For Southeastern Europe the figures are 188.50 per cent.

For feeblemindedness, Northwestern Europe shows 18.98 per cent for its quota fulfillment, while the South East stands at 33.02. The small numbers involved here make you realize two things—one, that many feebleminded people are in all probability taken care of at home, and two, that detection at time of entry is easier here than is the case with the insane. Russia-Finland, leads with 161 cases or 50.53 per cent, quota fulfillment. Nowhere else do the actual cases run above 100.

In the tables for epilepsy Great Britain stands at 145.56 per cent quota fulfillment, with 131 cases; Russia-Finland shows 117.19 per cent, and 150 cases, while Ireland with 108 cases presents a per cent of 108. There are other high per cents, but based in each case on a very small number of examples. The per cent for the North and West is 80.36, for the South and East, 89.04.

For the second generation, which Dr. Laughlin suggests, might be considered as "representative" of our immigration between 1880 and 1890,"[59] it is shown that, as to Insanity, Feeblemindedness, and Epilepsy, the following per cents exist in regard to those descended from two native born white parents, those from two foreign born parents, and lastly those who have one parent native, the other foreign born.

Quota fulfillments

	2 PARENTS NATIVE	2 PARENTS FOREIGN	PARENTS (1 NATIVE 1 FOREIGN)
Insanity	73 27	108.49	103.90
Feeblemindedness	107 70	165.39	190.27
Epilepsy	93 05	179 54	200.0

One other set of facts from the same table, is also valuable for review.

Quota fulfillments

	FOREIGN BORN	PARENTS FOREIGN BORN
Insane	225.76	108.49
Feebleminded	31.91	165.3
Epileptic	71.65	179.54

These are most interesting figures, and Prof. H. S. Jennings,[60] in his study of this report, brings up many challenging questions as to what meanings one may draw with fairness from them. In regard to a defect like insanity, which Prof. Jennings classes along with crime, pauperism and tuberculosis as a "mental, moral or physical breakdown," he asks if the foreign born who have come through the "soul searching" ordeal of immigration might not be expected to show a higher per cent, "even if the inheritance in the two cases be equal." He also mentions the fact that we do not have figures to show us in what proportions,[61] the native and the foreign born defectives find their way into the state and federal custodial institutions. He suggests that possibly figures from private institutions of a like nature, would show a reversal of the proportions of native born and foreign born. It may also be suspected that the foreign born might lead in cases kept at home.

As to the "second generation," Jennings points out the decided fall in the proportion of the insane, as compared with the proportions shown by the immigrants themselves, which is, as he says, "in harmony with the presumption that in them, it was due largely to the conditions involved in immigration."

On the other hand, in this second generation table, the figures for feeblemindedness and epilepsy rise to a higher level than that presented by the immigrants themselves, as well as to a higher level than that shown by the native born. These two defects therefore, which cannot be accounted for by difference in environment" yield, Jennings believes, "a positive indication of greater defectiveness in the immigrant stock." He gives some very interesting graphs showing certain of these facts in combination. His tables show the three highest groups in each defect, and finally the three nations that lead in all defects together. These run in this order:

> Ireland
> Russia-Finland
> Balkans

Jennings believes that the "general upshot, is of a character to discourage attempts to regulate immigration on the basis of race and nationality so far as Europeans are concerned."

His final conclusions[62] submitted both in person and in writing to the House Committee on Immigration and Naturalization, in January, 1924, state that the difference between the "Old" and the "New" immigration as set forth in the Laughlin study is not a sharply defined one; that the change from the 1910 basis to the 1890 one, would not reduce the numbers of European born defectives in governmental institutions; but would merely change the combinations, giving for instance, more insane, more epileptics, less feebleminded. Laughlin himself maintains that "the outstanding conclusion,"[63] making all allowances, is "that the recent immigrants, as a whole, present a higher percentage of inborn socially inadequate qualities than do the older stocks." His suggestions for remedy follow these lines: "Aside from the standards of soundness[64] for mind and body, at present required in the examination at Ellis Island, we must add a requirement for sound reputation, and also one for soundness of family stock." "A knowledge of family history is essential to keeping down the great percentage" of alien insane.

He asks for "a higher, or rather a more scientific personal standard for the admission of immigrants."[65] "The standards of mental ability and personality should be measured," he says, "by a series of modern psychological tests." These are interesting and definite suggestions. Some duly authenticated statement as to family and reputation would surely be of great import; with the data, in fairness to the individual, handled with much scientific understanding, if it is true, as some geneticists are coming to believe, that a study like that of the Juke family does not tell the whole story, and that some of those individual members might have had in them factors that under other circumstances would have produced different results.

In 1905 Dr. Salmon,[66] writing in regard to the foreign born insane in institutions, gives the figures as 1 in every 256 for the foreign born, as against 1 in every 765 for the native born. This estimate was based on figures for the year 1890. In 1903 he quotes the foreign born insane in institutions as standing at 31.5 per cent, while the per cent in the general population studied is but 13.5.

Of rather different import is an article by Dr. A. J. Rosanoff[67] who doubts that such unfavorable figures have absolute bearing as to interpretation of stock. He calls attention to the difference in age distribution, which exists between the native born and the foreign born, and to the difference in the proportion of city dwellers and country dwellers, which as well as race must have bearing on any interpretation. His most interesting point is where, in speaking of migrations, he quotes figures to show that these same general results are to be noticed in the case of Easterners migrating to the West, in the United States. In California, the natives of the state of New York who have gone to California have contributed 2.60 times as many admissions to the State Hospitals as have the native Californians. From his studies, Rosanoff draws the conclusion, that there is no evidence to show that there is a greater proneness toward mental disease in the foreign born, than in the native population.

Whether there is "greater proneness" or not, general opinion would probably hold, that while taking care of the insane "within," is necessary, it is perhaps equally necessary to devise the best possible means for preventing the entrance of those who come from "outside."

Prof. S. J. Holmes, again to quote a biologist, in surveying the question has these sentences:[68] "In regard to the immigrant, the question should be, not who can be proved bad enough to be sent away; but who can prove himself good enough to be admitted. The basis for selecting immigrants should be positive, not negative." This is followed by the suggestion that "matters would be helped if each newcomer were compelled to undergo a series of thorough mental tests, given in the language of the person." Holmes says further: "Despite present defects in the art of mental testing, and despite an occasional injustice to the immigrant, a test designed to exclude everyone up to and excluding the level of a high grade moron, would insure a much better result than we are now getting."

Dr. H. H. Goddard[69] writing in 1912, gives a brief survey as to "Feeble-mindedness and Immigration," where he reports on results gleaned from 16 different institutions. The foreign born here furnished but 4.5 per cent of the inmates. Of these, 95 cases were "morons who could not be expected to be recognized as they came through the 'Immigration Line.'" 231 cases were imbeciles, and 92 were idiots, but as the age at which they entered the country was unknown, "they may have been at that time 'infants in arms' who might easily have passed an officer." For 246 cases only, were facts as to the mental state of the parents known. Of this number 83 had parents one or both of whom were feebleminded. "This," Dr. Goddard says "seems to be a little more serious indictment against existing inspection," although of course it is not known of how high a grade these parents may have been.

This, then, brings to a close the description of the state of affairs existing as far as the administrative side of the Immigration question was concerned, at the time when this study of Ellis Island children was made.

[1] "Report of the Commissioner General of Immigration," 1922, p. 108. Fairchild, "Immigration," p. 62.
[2] Jenks and Lauck: "The Immigration Problem," p. 305, 1922 edition.
[3] Fairchild, Henry Pratt. "Immigration," p. 53. Jenks and Lauck, p. 365.

⁴ For a detailed account of the progress of legislation see: Jenks and Lauck, chap. xviii; Fairchild, chaps. iv, v, vi.

⁵ Fairchild, p. 122.

⁶ Fairchild, pp. 107–108. Jenks and Lauck, p. 375.

⁷ Fairchild, p. 115. Jenks and Lauck, p. 380.

⁸ For the existing laws, see: Government pamphlet, "Immigration Laws." Rules of May 1, 1917. Issue of August 1922.
For the 3 per cent law, see Government pamphlet, no. 5, 67th Congress, H. R. 4075.
For bill to limit to 2 per cent on the census of 1890, see H. R. 14273, Government pamphlet, February 9, 1923.

⁹ For full discussion of the law of 1917, see Jenks and Lauck, chap. xx, p. 423.

¹⁰ Jenks and Lauck, p. 436. Fairchild, p. 113.

¹¹ See text of law of 1917. See Fairchild, *op. cit.*, p. 107.

¹² Jenks and Lauck, *op. cit.*, p. 440.

¹³ At one time in the Ellis Island School there were three children of an insane mother, returned with her for deportation. It had not been possible to detect the insanity on arrival. The same children were at Ellis Island the year before. The great responsibility of that family did not belong to this country. One might be glad that all were to go back to relatives in Europe; and yet regret that in some way it had not been possible to stop them at the beginning. In such cases the idea of "authenticated records," before the stamping of a passport, may help.

¹⁴ Immigration Report, 1922, p. 104, note 1.

¹⁵ Jenks and Lauck, *op. cit.*, p. 445. Immigration law of 1917, Government pamphlet, p. 11, 7th edition, August 1922.

¹⁶ Immigration law of 1917, Government pamphlet, p. 16. As to question of Payment see: "Hearings before the House Committee on Immigration, December 1923, January 1924, Serial 1A. Government Printing Office, 78952, p. 623.

¹⁷ Immigration law of 1917, Government pamphlet, p. 18.

¹⁸ For text in regard to "Illiteracy Test," see Jenks and Lauck, p. 425. See also Immigration Report, 1917, p. xii: xiv.

¹⁹ Jenks and Lauck, p. 410.

²⁰ Jenks and Lauck, p. 428.

²¹ A physician, who for ten years has done mental examining at Ellis Island, has said that directly the law went into effect he noticed differences in the material arriving.
See also Public Health Service Report, 1917, p. 157, for the same general statement.
See also *Congressional Record*, 60, no. 64, p. 3555.
The writer was shown in Italy an answer sent from America to a letter asking about this test. A lawyer had been consulted, and a sample of the kind of thing necessary for reading had been sent back. There was probably no dishonesty in this regard, and even if there were, the strain

under which the test is taken, and the fact that no one can tell just what sentence the inspector will ask to have read, would militate against its being successful.

A most interesting case of shell-shock, detected by no other means, was found out at the time of the illiteracy test.

[22] See Jenks and Lauck, op. cit., p. 429.

[23] Report of Commissioner General of Immigration, 1917, p. xiv, xii.

[24] For description see Immigration Report, 1917, p. xiv.

[25] Once before a Board of Inquiry when a debarred "illiterate" woman was asked if she wished to appeal (which is always done) she answered that she did. When the formal paper was given her to sign, she put a cross for her signature. The presiding officer, through the interpreter, said, "But I thought you said that you could write your name." The woman said that she could. "Then do it," said the inspector, "The fact may help you in Washington." The alien's interests are carefully protected.

[26] Immigration Report, 1920, p. 13.

[27] For total immigration admission figures see Immigration Report, 1922, p. 101.

[28] Congressional Record, February 14, 1921, p. 3372.

[29] The "3 per cent law" went into effect June 3, 1921. See Immigration Report, 1921, p. 16.

[30] Arranged from figures in Immigration Reports of 1920, pp. 96–97; 1921, pp. 34-35-36; 1922, pp. 32-33-34; 1923, pp. 48-49-50.

[31] Congressional Record, February 14, 1921, p. 3372.

[32] Immigration Reports, 1922, p. 101, and pp. 112–113; 1923, p. 48 and p. 128.

[33] Immigration Report, 1922, pp. 117–118.

[34] Immigration Report, 1921, p. 16; 1922, pp. 3–9.

[35] Jenks and Lauck, op. cit., p. 448.

[36] Immigration Report, 1922, pp. 3–18.

[37] Government pamphlet, House Resolution 14273.

[38] Commissioner Husband in the New York Tribune for April 4, 1923, is quoted as saying that he did not think "that the demand voiced by an element among industrial leaders for less restriction, on the ground that the country needs laborers, was representative of the sentiment among employers." He asserted that in touring the country he found most of the men of the generation that soon will provide the business heads of the nation, desirous of having curbs put on immigration from the south and east of Europe. The Commissioner here added (speech before the Civitan Club in New York City) that "contrary to the general belief, neither organized labor nor organized capital had any weight in the last five years in shaping the Immigration policy, but that Congress had been acting on what it believed to be the sentiment of the United States as a whole.

For congestion under present 20 per cent a month crowding see Public Health Service Report, 1922, p. 203.

[39] *Op. cit.*, note 38.

[40] *Congressional Record*, February 14, 1921, p. 3372.

[41] Baltimore *Sun*, April 18, 1923, vol. 172, no. 130.

See also article by Professor Henry P. Fairchild on "Immigration and Labor" in answer to Mr. Gary's contention as to labor shortage, *New York Times*, Sunday, April 29, 1923.

[42] *Congressional Record*, February 14, 1921, p. 3367; vol. 60, no. 64, p. 3550.

[43] Jenks and Lauck, *op. cit.*, 5th edition, p. 46.

[44] *Seattle Times*, October 23, 1921.

[45] Baltimore *Evening Sun*, April 19, 1923.

[46] U. S. Public Health Service Report, 1914, p. 196.

[47] U. S. Public Health Service Report, 1916, p. 195. See also report for 1921, p. 232.

In 1921, because of fear of typhus infection, 21 principal foreign ports are reported as being so covered.

[48] See Baltimore *Evening Sun*, April 19, 1923.

[49] Commissioner Husband speaking in Arundel Hall, Baltimore, Wednesday, November 21, 1923, said that "counting" on the other side probably would be part of the law enacted by the "next Congress." He reminded the audience, however, that need for medical examination here would always exist.

[50] *New York Tribune*, April 4, 1923.

[51] The "peak" of immigration figures (1907 = 1,285,349).

[52] House Resolution 476, Government pamphlet.

[53] "Analysis of America's Modern Melting Pot." Harry H. Laughlin. Government Printing Office Publication, Serial 7C, no. 33555, November 21, 1922.

[54] Law of 1917 (Government pamphlet). Also Commissioner General Husband. Speech, Arundel Club, Baltimore, Wednesday, November 21, 1923.

[55] *Op. cit.*, note 53, p. 729.

[56] "Undesirable Aliens." H. S. Jennings. *The Survey*, December 15, 1923, p. 309.

[57] *Op. cit.*, 56.

[58] Quoted as example by Professor Jennings, Biology Seminary, October 23, 1923.

[59] *Op. cit.*, note 53, p. 753.

[60] *Op. cit.*, note 56.

[61] Hearings before House Committee on Immigration, Serial 1A, no. 78952, p. 540, for criticism of the Laughlin Report on Statistical Grounds by Dr. John M. Gillman.

[62] Hearings before House Committee on Immigration, no. 78952, pp. 511–518.

[63] *Op. cit.*, note 53, p. 755.
[64] *Op. cit.*, note 53, p. 756.
[65] *Op. cit.*, note 53, p. 757.
[66] "The Diagnosis of Insanity in Immigrants." Assist. Surg. Thomas W. Salmon. U. S. Public Health Service Report, 1905, pp. 271–278.
[67] Rosenoff, A. J. "Manual of Psychiatry," 1920, pp. 17–18. "Some Neglected Phases of Immigration in Relation to Insanity." *American Journal Insanity*, lxxii, July 1915.

See also Waldman, Morris D. "The Alien as a Public Charge with Particular Reference to the Insane." *Annual Report, New York State Board of Charities*, vol. 1, Albany, New York, 1913.

See also, Pollock, H. M. "A Statistical Study of the Foreign Born Insane." *New York State Hospital Bulletin*, April 1912.

Charles M. Burr, M.D. "The Foreign Born Insane." *Journal American Medical Association*, lxii, pp. 25–27.

James V. May, M.D. "Mental Diseases," 1922. Chap. ix, "Immigration and Mental Diseases." Here the author tries to show how differing racial characteristics seem to call forth differing mental diseases. He gives interesting tables by races taken from the records of the New York State Hospitals. The per cents of admissions show that the 3 highest races in 1916, 1917, 1918, 1919, 1920, run each time in the following order: Irish, German, Hebrew.

[68] "Studies in Evolution and Eugenics." S. J. Holmes, pp. 212–213.
[69] "Feeble-mindedness and Immigration." H. H. Goddard. *The Training School Bulletin*, vol. 9, 1912–13, pp. 91–94.

CHAPTER IV

For the better understanding of the reports[1] which will follow, it is perhaps well now to describe, with certain comments, the actual procedure at Ellis Island, the successor to Castle Garden as the Immigrant Station in New York Harbor. That Castle Garden still lives, however, must not be overlooked; because many times in mental examinations, in answer to the question, "What place is this?" the answer comes very promptly, "Castle Garden," and is counted as correct.

In a book entitled "Immigration and the Commissioners of Emigration of the State of New York," by "Friedrich Kapp,[2] one of the said Commissioners," published in 1870, there are to be found "Rules and Regulations of the Emigrant Landing Depot, Castle Garden," which in their headings show themselves to be the ancestors of the system of today.

I quote them:

1. Emigrants
. 2. Boarding House Keepers.
3. Missionaries.
4. General Rules. [For the government of Landing Depot.]
5. Rules and Regulations. [For government of Information Office for friends of arriving emigrants.]
6. Rules and Regulations. [For government of the Labor Exchange and Intelligence Offices.]
7. R.R. Department.
8. Exchange Brokers.
9. Restaurant and Bread Stands.
10. Wash Rooms.
11. Hospitals.

These were the groupings of the regulations of May 18, 1867.

They might with little change of wording and with slight extension be used today. The main administration building contains aside from its offices, the reception station for the Medical Division, as well as that of the Immigration section proper. It has detention rooms—the day quarters with their outdoor porches, and the dormitories. It has dining rooms, it has temporary detention rooms, and rooms for special inquiry hearings. It hums with the work of railroad offices, and money exchanging, of welfare societies, of meeting places for relations who come to take in charge the admitted immigrant, or to visit the one detained. Three neighboring buildings house the large hospital which during the fiscal year ending June 30, 1923, had a grand total of 11,057 admissions.[3] Yet there is sore need of greater extension still, for the carrying on of the immense amount of work that must be done. Commissioner Curran,[4] in a public statement, has referred to an appropriation of over $2,000,000 which he has requested of Congress through the Commissioner General of Immigration. The suggested improvements begin with an enlarging of the island itself.

The Commissioner states that the Ellis Island receipts for head tax, steamship fines, and detention charges, totaled over $3,000,000, while the expenses of the island were but slightly over $1,200,000, leaving a profit tor the year ending June 30, 1923, of over $1,800,000. It must be remembered, however, that smaller stations probably show no such proportionate balance, and that the money question for the Immigration system as a whole, would present quite different results.

That much criticism of Ellis Island has come from outside is true, the most notable example being the published report of the British Ambassador to the United States.[5] Yet the fact remains, as to British Immigration, that while according to the figures of the 1922 report,[6] the United Kingdom sent to this country but 42,670 persons, or 55.2 per cent of its allotted 77,342, the year 1923 saw the quota exhausted in May, and for 1924[7] it was practically filled as early as November.

In commenting on this fact, Commissioner General Husband said, that last year 63 per cent of the incoming immigrants were of the "old stock," with the remainder being from the South East of Europe. This, he said, was a realization of what Congress had hoped—that a holding back of the "new," would encourage the old to come. That other factors, aside from the quota law enter here, is, of course, true; but the law surely has great bearing on the results. If there had been no restrictions, Commissioner Husband declared, we should probably have had the largest British immigration for forty years.

To return to the consideration of the island, we have then, to remember that the hospital at one time may contain in its various sections, its hundreds, and the detention station its "more than a thousand." These numbers in combination with the many workers in all divisions, make of this "Immigrant Station" almost a town of its own. In considering what happens, when the tide sweeps through, and the sifting process works, these numbers have always to be remembered. No steamship company may send its passengers to the Island, until the Commissioner gives the word that he is ready to receive them. If too many ships arrive at one time, they come in turn, and until its turn arrives the steamship company has to care for its own.

It will perhaps serve best to explain what happens, if we follow an immigrant through. He is brought to the island from his steamship on a barge—one of several operated by a company which is in charge of this transportation, and whose agent has an office on the island. It is supposedly made clear to him that his baggage, with certain exceptions, may be checked if he so desires.[8] That he often, in fact you might say, "generally," does not so desire to any great extent, is due to his own customary methods of procedure, rather than to lack of given opportunity.

As the barges draw near the landing place, let us suppose that an "intensive" examination has been decided upon, in the Medical Division. No steamship company can know just how any given examination will be run, as the physicians themselves do not know in any given case, until the word is "passed" by the Chief Line Officer. From the barges then, usually in single file, which is surveyed most critically by the Chief Line Officer himself as it advances, in times when he wishes to watch for some particular danger, the immigrants walk with their ever present baggage into a large room where benches stretch in lines on all sides.

People, here again, often criticize the partitions or pens, as they call them, which are used to make the immigrants go in the right direction, or to keep them in the appropriate place. If these critics had once tried to stop a stampede into the *wrong* place, when 15 different languages would have been needed to make all understand, and when there was no way of knowing which language would cause the desired effect on the leading man, they would need no explanations of the great usefulness of all partitions, not only for the convenience of the examiners, but for accomplishing the greatest saving in the immigrant's time and comfort. If two ship loads are to be in the waiting room at once, the officer in charge uses great care to keep them apart, by moving benches to act as fences; for counting and lists have always to be reckoned with.

One feels conscious always in the workings of our Immigration system, that it is not the work of one time, or of one man. It is a growth, and day by day, "this" is tried and abandoned, "that" tried and kept. The only written signs anywhere in this whole process, are those on the toilet room doors, and they prove the utter uselessness of printed signs, for some language in them has to come first, and anyone not understanding that first word, takes it for granted that the sign is in English, and looks no further. For the most part too, spoken language is not used either in guiding this carefully planned advance, as the line starts its progress. The barred off pathways, and motioning guards have been found most effective for the movement of the mass.

When the line begins to move for the waiting room, it passes through a gate one at a time, when each landing ticket is stamped, or if a certain "number" is to be held up for some reason or other, it may be here picked out. Those who pass through are at once in another smaller waiting room, where each is made to deposit all his baggage—men here, women there—and where the sixty men and forty women and children, or whatever number it may be that has been passed through, sit to wait for the next move, in groups of twenty or twenty-five, into the physicians' examining rooms.

Now, of course, this is a time of tension, and specially so for the women, in that the children, who always go with the women, are restless—often hungry and fretful.[9] This causes added worry to the mother, who is herself, many times, not used to taking initiative. For this reason, the women doctors have a rather different problem in this intensive examination, from that found by the men. If one child cries, others cry. The skill necessary to obviate this state of affairs, the quick change from one kind of examination to another, when necessary for reasons of quiet, the letting children alone till the disturbance ·has subsided, and all this in crowded quarters, where in spite of the fact that through different doctors and different attendants, many languages are available, at certain times signs are the sole means of communication, makes a very special technique a necessity, as well as medical skill, and a generous understanding of human beings. One realizes the force of a sentence found in the "Regulation for the Medical Inspection of Aliens:"[10] "Knowledge of racial characteristics in physique, costume, and behavior are important in this inspection procedure." An understanding, though firm physician, does much to calm an entire family or room full, and this is true even when really a certificate of a specially troublesome kind may have been given.

Here again in the case of certification, the wisdom of experience is shown; for the doctors do *not* explain to the people to whom a "certificate" of some form or other is given—perhaps for hospitalization, perhaps for a Class C defect which has to do with ability to earn a living, perhaps a card showing that further mental examination is called for. Explanation would, of course, be impossible, and the great skill that all workers at Ellis Island have developed in avoiding, where necessary, direct answers to questions, is very remarkable. I have heard this criticised; but when you see the difficulties[11] that direct answering may bring, the wisdom is understood. The medical division can not answer questions as to what the Immigration Inspectors will do; the examining Doctor can not say what the Hospital will decide; the complicated machinery, to work well, really must work fairly "silently," and sometimes one comes to believe that the mixture of language which halts conversation, is perhaps a factor most conducive to a successful and speedy working of the system.

After the medical examination is over, an immigrant may pass out quickly, gather up his luggage, have his card inspected and stamped, and go directly to the Immigration authorities; or if something is physically or mentally wrong, he may be sent to the mental room for further examination or to the hospital. This part of the proceeding seems the most difficult. If one member of a family is sent through a door into the "hospital" waiting room, for instance, while the rest, with cards quickly stamped, are sent suddenly through another door, which leads them on to the Immigration inspection, it is, of course, an anxious and difficult time. "Not to know" is almost unbearable, yet granting that, it seems that the situation is carefully handled. The family, who have passed on, as they are "incomplete," are detained on the Immigration floor, as those "together," pass on to the inspectors together naturally. In time they will know that they are to wait in the detention rooms, till the sick member's case is settled, that if the sick child has gone to the hospital the mother may go to her the next day at visiting hour, etc. I feel that a Medical Social Service worker here, of the type that the Medical Division has in the Hospitals, could help in this hardship, yet the delicacy of handling a "half way through" case without mistake would be enormous, and the wide range of language necessary could never centre in any one person; for here at least words would be necessary.[12] It is particularly dangerous ground too, as it is at the border line between the Medical and the Immigration side, which work together so well, apparently, because of this strictly separated and carefully respected allotment of jurisdiction.

I should like at this point to say a word as to the mental examinations, which are of extreme interest.[13] Dr. Mullan, who writes so clearly and authoritatively on this question, reminds us of the need of racial knowledge here. If an Englishman should react to questions in the manner of an Irishman, his lack of mental balance would be suspected. No physician can do the examining of this kind at an Immigrant Station without having a knowledge far beyond his psychiatric knowledge. In talking with a surgeon who has been doing this work for many years, one is always in a state of amazement at the amount of background he has gained, which makes things intelligible to him, which are entirely unknown and unrecognized by one without this skill.

If the immigrant,[14] because of fear or fatigue, or excitement, seems unable to show his capacity, such as it may be, on this arrival day—he is sent by the physicians, after trial, to the detention rooms, to wait until another day. Then the examination is taken up again, the next day, and the next, if necessary, and soon until the doctor is convinced that there is no need of detention, or that a certificate must be given. In this last case, decision is never rendered without the judgment and signature of two physicians.[15]

Feeblemindedness, although it is lowered at our stations, because of the greater care of the steamship companies in their examinations,[16] because of the deterring effect of the "illiteracy" test, and because of the lessened numbers brought about by the 3 per cent law, is still a menace that is most carefully and necessarily watched for.

These mental examinations average about five hundred people[17] a month. This number, of course, does not show the number of examinations any given individual may have; for any one of the "500" may need two or three or four examinations, or more—as the case may be. It also does not show the re-examinations that are constantly going on, for people who have appealed, and who at intervals are brought back to Ellis Island. The number of "certified" cases as they appear in the various reports can therefore give but little idea of the scope of the mental work that is actually done.

Now come the individual cases—a sampling of those that were watched by the writer. First it must be remembered that from observing these examinations you learn much that is quite apart from things mental. An Irishman was turned aside on the line, which is to be described later, and sent to the mental rooms. Confusion of any kind can not be handled in the line. Instant turning aside to the mental rooms, when any question arises, has to be the procedure. "Why were you sent in here?" said the doctor. "Because I did the arithmetic wrong that the doctor gave me," the man answered instantly—a good beginning. "What was it?" said the doctor. The man answered instantly again, "I said 21 + 22 were 42, and I ought to have said 43." The man was a steel worker. "Do you drink beer?" said the doctor with a purpose. "No," said the man, "I am a teetotaler." "You drink only oatmeal and water then?" was the doctor's next speech, to which the man said "Yes." Then came questions as to his Irish farm, as to the relative value of the English and the

Irish acre, all of which the man handled so intelligently that he was not further held. Now it is this sort of preliminary questioning that shows the fund of knowledge necessary for even the beginning of mental work with aliens. This approach on the part of the doctor establishes a relation which nothing else can do, and as the emotional state plays such a large part, the importance of this preliminary state of adjustment cannot be over emphasized. To know who drinks oatmeal and water and who does not, may seem a little thing; but its effects may be far reaching.

Also the things that may cause wrong answers have to be watched for very carefully. In the middle of an examination where a girl was asked the question as to which she would throw overboard, bread or money, if out at sea in a small boat which must be lightened, the answer came "The bread." The doctor said nothing; but very slowly told the story again. Instantly the girl said. "Oh I didn't understand before—I was so full of that big boat that I have just been on, that I never noticed the little boat part. I should, of course throw over the gold." Now that was not a changing of the answer because of the suspicion that something was wrong. It was a real lack of understanding because of the omnipresence of that big boat. A hasty decision as to the girl's mental processes would surely in this case not have shown the facts.

What an individual does when waiting for an examination is also a matter of great interest. They may walk, or sit stupidly, or sit with a most alert interest in everything that is happening in the waiting room around them. One girl slept. That does not often happen. The process is not conducive to sleep. Three cases may be enough to serve our purpose.

Case I. Yiddish boy. (Russian.) Age, fourteen years. Never has been to school. Counted from 1 to 20. Did Sequin form board, after attempts at forcing in unlikely places. Imbecile Form Board: No.

The next day the boy came a second time with his mother, and the examination this time was carried on through an interpreter. Two physicians instead of one were present.

The mother was first questioned, and that the boy had not talked till he was ten was brought out. That he had not gone to school, she said, was due to the "Bolshevists." She admitted that her three other children, still in Russia, were brighter than this boy. They had gone to school.

All this showed that the family knew quite well that there was a difficulty in the case of this, the only boy. So many times the defective child is left at home with relatives, and then brought over if possible when the weight of establishment already completed in the United States, may be an important factor, the family hopes, in all deliberations! Why this boy was brought first, was not clear.

This time the examination proceeded as follows:

Counting from one to twenty: Correct.

Twenty to one: Failed.

One to twelve: Correct.

Twelve to one: Failed.

The months? Not known. (This is, of course, often true in normal cases.)

Digits: Failed. If 5:7:9 were given, the boy would say 9.

The imbecile form board: Correct this time on repetition. Failed the day before.

Knox cubes: Absolutely at a loss. After 4 repetitions of a simple series (of 3) he finally did it once.

Healy frame: Correct.

Healy frame: Repeated. Correct.

Sequin form board: Correct.

In addition could do:

3	3
3	4
5	4
6	5
6	6

But could not do 6 7 or anything beyond.

Morning or afternoon? Answered "Afternoon."

Why did he say "Afternoon?" Answered "Because I have eaten."

Colors: Knew red only.

Aesthetic card (Binet): 1 Right. Seemed to point as happened.

Missing parts (Binet): No idea.

Weights (Binet): No idea.

Watch? Knew name.

Time? Did not know.

How many legs has a dog? Correct.

How many legs has a horse? Correct.

How many legs have both? "Six."

Had he ever seen a cow? Yes.

Was it the same as a horse? Yes.

Questioned again, said "No."

Well how is it different? "A cow has two horns." Then, "A cow has eyes and a horse has eyes."

During these examinations the boy had a most pained open-mouthed expression, yet at times, as when he was at work on the form boards, he showed much more concentration than might have been expected. He was later certified as an imbecile.

Case II. Polish woman of thirty. Schooling had lasted two months and no more.

Counting 20 to 1: Slow but correct.
Days of the week: Correct.
Months: Gave only ten.
Digits: Gave 5 correctly.[18]
Healy frame: Very good.
Second time, Healy frame: Extremely fast.
Sequin form board: Good.
Knox cubes: 5 correct.
Washing steps: Correct.
Why? "Because that is the order."
Why again? "Because they would get dirty if you did it the other way." This is interesting to me, because "rule of thumb" in so many cases with peasants, seems a fact not to be questioned; but to be accepted.
Boat: Which throw overboard: food or gold—"Gold is dearer than bread; but doesn't know." Told to decide. Then said: "Gold; because life is most dear."
Girl cut in ten pieces: "It must be someone else—she couldn't do it herself."
Fire, which would she throw out, the mattress or the lamp?. Answer: "I should leave everything to save my life. When told to say one or the other she answered: "I should carry that lamp."
Donkey and Little Boy Story: Answer: "Maybe the donkey kicked him."

This woman was passed. Through the entire examination she was perfectly undisturbed, with a sort of "un-awake" poise. Her husband worked in a factory. He had worked in a brick yard. She had two children. She accepted life as well as wished to keep it!

Case III. Greek boy of eight,—that is really just beyond his seventh birthday. He had never been to school.

He was turned aside by the Chief Line Officer on sight, as he was passing into the waiting rooms. At first when asked to count, he did well. Then he cried and repeated over and over again what the Dr. had said. An interpreter was sent for; but still things were at a deadlock, and the boy was detained for a later examination. The next morning the continuance of the examination came. Again the boy, though urged by his mother,

and by the interpreter, could not seem to talk. The appearance was of great stage fright: Finally the child counted from 1 to 20.
Counting backwards 20 to 1: Failed.
Counting backwards 10 to 1: Failed.
Digits. He repeated six.
Colors: No answer.
Aesthetic judgment (Binet): All wrong.
Then a sort of panic came, and all operations stopped, to be taken up again the next day. The doctor had the interpreter explain in a most kindly way to the boy, that he was holding up the entire family; that tomorrow he must do better.
The next day he came again. He did the Imbecile form board instantly. He did the Healy Frame fast, and smiled. He did the weights (Binet) right, twice in succession without difficulty. He answered as to missing parts correctly with one exception.
Cubes: Four were done with some difficulty.
Right hand: Correct.
Left ear: Correct.
Fingers on one hand? "Five" instantly.
Fingers on two hands? Instantly, correct.
Toes on one foot? Correct.
Fingers and toes together? Correct.
He was told that if he had done all this on the first day, he would not have kept mother waiting, and passed.

That the extreme terror of the first examination could settle into the enjoyment of the last, seemed, without the seeing, such an impossibility that even when watching it happening you could not recognize the "two" boys as "one." Such a case is a warning.

To watch the examinations day after day, gives one a view of thought processes not his own perhaps; but certainly just as workable. It makes one realize very strongly what some of the qualities and conditions, good and bad, are, which start individuals to migrating. One is forced too, to think of the individual tests, as perhaps they might not be thought of under more "even" conditions. For instance—after watching in the Knox Cube test, the almost imperceptible swaying which goes on when the Doctor makes his moves, an observer gets to feeling a sort of "against the tide" motion, that would never come if the established procedure were to have both experimenter and subject facing in the same direction, and with the cubes before them, instead of having them opposite to each other, with the cubes between, as the present instructions insist.

Now we shall return to the general examinations again. So far "intensive examinations" only have been described—the procedure that a lessened immigration has made possible to a greater extent than in the past. The other system of inspection in use, is the "line inspection," which has been, up to now, but casually referred to. In this procedure, the immigrant, on arrival, with hat off, but unfortunately with luggage in hand, passes down a line so controlled in its movement, that the physicians may see the immigrant both walking toward them, and also if they so choose, walking away. Four of these lines may be running at one time, a given immigrant in each case, having to pass two physicians.

The first, looks at him in general, talks to him (or at least makes the immigrant say something), makes him drop everything and hold out his hands, and if suspicious in any way, marks him for an intensive examination. If marked, the immigrant is passed without comment by the second physician and guided by the attendant into the passage leading to the medical examining rooms. If on the other hand the immigrant is not chalk marked by the first physician, he comes before the second, usually a senior officer, who particularly examines his eyes, and then looks at him in general for as long as he may choose, to pick up anything that may have escaped notice before. If the immigrant is marked on this second inspection, he goes to the examining rooms for careful examination as does the one marked by the first examining physician; but if he escapes marking in both cases, he is then free to pass directly to the Immigration floor.

Here too, in this process, we get separation of families, and from watching this line day after day, one comes to the conclusion that often when there is outward sign of emotion, one member of the family being sent down a separate passage to the Medical Rooms while the other members go their way, the cause is often traced, not to the main feature of separation and anxiety, but to some small and little expected thing.

One notices also with interest, something that must, in all probability, have been planned, though no one seemed to know of its direct planning. At the separation point, where one way leads to the Immigration floor, and the other, parallel to it for a distance, leads to the Doctor's rooms, the wire dividing partition is covered with canvas; but after a few yards, the canvas covering is discontinued. Now at the time of separation, there is a shock, and people stop. Moved on by the attendant, as long as the canvas keeps them from seeing their companion, they "move on," to stop at once where the removal of the canvas gives a chance to talk, and to pass belongings back and forth. This means that the passage is kept from being blocked, and yet that a chance is given for communication, before the pathways finally separate. It is in working out, a most simple way of accomplishing very necessary ends, and is an example of the kind of growth to fit circumstances that is everywhere apparent.

After the Medical Inspection comes the Immigration Inspection, where the groups and individuals as they arrive on the "Inspection Floor," are directed down a lane of benches, leading to the Inspector, who has the particular manifest sheet containing their names. A family not complete, as we have seen, waits. Here too there are interpreters, and attendants to help, and the lines often move very quickly. The illiteracy test must be passed at the Inspector's desk, and the necessary questions must be answered. If this is done successfully, the immigrant passes out to the New York ferry, where Traveller's Aid representatives wait to help him, or into the railroad room, where he is transferred by a special boat to his railroad line, and there met and put on his train, or to a temporary detention room, if he is not to be discharged from the island until he is put into the hands of friends. From this room, which is used most particularly to guard women travelling alone, no one leaves the island, until the person calling, has satisfied an Inspector, that he is the expected husband, or father, or brother as the case may be.

Then there are those who do not pass out. An individual may be held until his case is passed upon by a "Board of Special Inquiry." These "Boards" consist of three inspectors, and they are usually served by an interpreter and a messenger.

An immigrant held for such inquiry, is not allowed to see his friends, until the inquiry is over; but he may have his own necessary witnesses at the inquiry itself. In a separate room, before these three "judges" then, first of all the immigrant makes his statement, or it is drawn from him by questioning. In front of the judges, are all the papers in the case, of which a brief summary is usually given at the very outset. After the judges are satisfied that they have all the facts that the immigrant can give them, the messenger summons the witnesses from an adjoining waiting room.

This is a most interesting moment to watch; because the sister may be looking at the brother for the first time in many years, or a woman, for the first time, may be seeing the man that she has come thousands of miles to marry. Yet in this moment, there is no break in the proceedings. The immigrant is not allowed to speak to the witness—the witness sometimes does not even glance at the bench, where the immigrant is sitting. All thoughts center on the inquiry itself. Personal thoughts have no place. But if the verdict is favorable, and the word of admission is briefly announced, witnesses and immigrants, in the midst of tears and embraces, may have to be swept out of the inquiry room together, by the messenger who has to clear the decks instantly for the oncoming case.

When a favorable decision can not be given, the witnesses may be questioned merely, and depart again, waiting for further consideration of the case. If the decision is an adverse one, the immigrant then and there is asked if he wishes to appeal, and if he does, the appeal is made ready for him to sign. Decisions here rest solely on the law. Any exceptions to the law, must come from higher authorities. That makes for the successful working out of the general scheme, yet this is the stage that the newspapers often use, for those heart rending stories, which in their final settlement (*have*) not separated mothers from babies or student husbands from accompanying wives.

If there is not this "Special Inquiry" as the cause for detention, there may be detention to wait for money, or for the recovery of a sick child, or there may be the detention until a steamer sails to take the immigrant back to a foreign port again, if he is mandatorially excludable from disease or from character, or if he is over quota, or likely to become a public charge, or if he infringes the rules as to "contract labor," or in some other way has not the right to enter the United States.

If an immigrant is detained, he often settles down to a certain acceptance of the fact. Community interests grow up. The discomforts, which of course are present, are so much emphasized that it seems well to speak of this. New friendships are made, the various nationals tend to gather in little groups on the porches or in the day rooms. School, Sunday services, occasional concerts, the bathing of babies in the nursery, visits to the hospital, receiving visits from friends, the ever recurring three meals a day, all serve to make a life that is much more filled with variety than some of these same lives have ever known before.

Where many have never previously suffered from such crowded conditions, others have never before had so much done for them. Clothes are furnished, sewing is given out, and all the various societies[19] at work at the island, lend themselves to the furnishing of any necessary and possible help.

Then too we must remember that if one woman is bitter because of the untidy habits of some of her neighbors, these same neighbors, hard working mothers of large families, may be looking at her with scorn because of a moral defect which means exclusion. Even deportation seems not always the unbearable experience that many writers think it to be.

A theoretical estimate of immigration usually lacks much in an understanding of these various and interlaced parts. Out of this atmosphere, then, came the children of whom I shall speak. In this atmosphere, whatever further advance, in the process of selection is deemed wise, will have to be developed.

[1] For descriptions of procedure at Ellis Island see:

(1) "Regulations Governing the Medical Inspection of Aliens." 1917: Govt. Printing Office, Miscellaneous Publication No. 5.

(2) "Manual of the Mental Examination of Aliens." 1918, Govt. Printing Office, Miscellaneous Publication No. 18.

(3) "The Mentality of the Arriving Immigrant." E. H. Mullan. 1917, Govt. Printing Office, Public Health Bulletin 90.

°(4) "Mental Examination of Immigrants. Administration and Line Inspection at Ellis Island." E. H. Mullan. 1917, Govt. Printing Office: Reprint No. 398 from the Public Health Service Report.

(5) "The Medical Examination of Mentally Defective Aliens, Its Scope and Limitations." L. L. Williams, M.D. American Journ. of Insanity, 71, no. 2, pp. 257–268, October 1914.

(6) Public Health Service, Annual Report 1910, p. 166. Description by Dr. Mullan, writing from Montreal, as to the detection of mental defectives.

(7) "Medical Inspection of Aliens at Ellis Island with Special Reference to the Examination of Women and Children." Mary T. Mernin M.D. A. A. Surgeon U. S. P. H. S. *Medical Woman's Journal*, vol. xxxi, no. 6, June 1924, pp. 172-175.

(8) "Imported Americans." Broughton Brandenburg.

2 "Immigration and the Commissioners of Emigration of the State of New York." Friedrich Kapp. New York, 1870 (The Nation Press).

3 Annual Report, U. S. Public Health Service, 1923, p. 188.

4 *New York Times*, December 22, 1923.

5 See *New York Times*, August 16, 1923, for text.

6 Report Commissioner General of Immigration, 1922, p. 5.

7 Speech by Commissioner General Husband. November 21, 1923, Arundel Hall, Baltimore.

8 Odd things often happen in regard to luggage. What is checked on one side of an official may be picked up, tag and all, by the immigrant, and carried off, on the other side, unless great care is used. That such a procedure offers difficulties, when later the check is produced, can easily be understood.

9 Often when the children are hungry, it is due to the fact that owing to the excitement of boarding the barges, and through various fears, the mother has not given them breakfast even though breakfast is provided.

10 "Medical Inspection of Aliens," p. 19, *op. cit.*, note 1.

11 A boy, while waiting to be summoned to the examination room, once asked if it were true that it would take him days to get through Ellis Island. He was of a nationality that had just been making complaints against the treatment of its nationals at Ellis Island, and the first impulse was to say: "No, it doesn't take days. The stories that you hear are exaggerated." With the usual caution, the answer given was, "If you are all right in every way, you go through very quickly." The boy went on into the examining room, and in the next hospital train that went out, he led the line. Though lack of direct answering is sometimes thought "unfeeling," it seems much kinder in the long run, than voluminous but perhaps false information. Sometimes, of course, lack of a helpful answer is due to irritability or fatigue on the part of the guard; but it seems unusually seldom that this is the case in the midst of much possible provocation. To distinguish the moment when everything must stop until a full answer to a question is given (as when a woman's baby has died, and she doesn't know just what has happened) takes a certain sort of ever alert comprehending attention, and in the midst of swamping numbers, cases needing attention may pass unheeded for a while; but they are sure to be found out in time, and then great kindness shown.

12 There is great danger of overemphasizing the hardship, for many times a mother is dissolved in tears over separation from a baby that is trotting off to the care that the hospital will give, most happily. After having seen the two the next day, you realize that at least the particular strain referred to is but temporary, however great an anxiety it may

develop into, in serious cases of illness. That, however, is a very different question which natives at home, as well as aliens travelling, must at times go through.

13 "Mental Examinations of Immigrants," p. 8, *op. cit.*, note 1.

14 An old woman from Macedonia who, when first brought into the examination room, did nothing but pray, paying practically no attention to questions asked her through the interpreter, on the next day, after a night of sleep, and after talking with her family whom she joined in the detention rooms, answered promptly and well, the questions that the doctor asked, and did with sufficient readiness such performance tests as she was asked to do. Great care is taken not to judge in haste.

15 For case histories see: "Manual for the Mental Examination of Aliens," pp. 72–109, *op. cit.*, note 1.

See also "Mental Examination of Immigrants," E. H. Mullan, pp. 8–9, *op. cit.*, note 1.

16 Commissioner Husband in a speech in Baltimore on November 21, 1923, cited some figures which were gathered, as well as could be, over a given time, to show how many people were turned back by steamship companies in comparison with those refused during the same time by the immigration authorities. 50,000 were turned back by the companies in the specified time, while only 6000 or 7000 were so turned, by the machinery of immigration. Fines are a cause of caution for the steamship companies.

17 Figures given personally by Dr. Loughran of Ellis Island.

18 In regard to digits, Dr. Loughran said that he found very few Italians who could give six, while the English, the Scotch, and the Germans could get six easily. It seems probable that the actual length of the words themselves (in some languages a factor) could not in these cases enter into the question.

19 The list of 1922, shows 19 different societies which have representatives doing work with the immigrants.

VITA

The writer was born in Brookline, Massachusetts, on February 26, 1877. After college preparation at the Brookline High School, she entered Radcliffe College in Cambridge, Massachusetts, where in 1899, she received the A.B. degree "magna cum laude." In 1907–1908, she was a student at the American School for Classical Studies in Rome. In 1912 she took the A.M. degree in Latin and Archaeology at Columbia University. For two spring terms, she has gone to lectures at the University of Rome. During the academic years 1921–1922, 1922–1923, and for the first half of the academic year 1923–1924, she has been enrolled as a graduate student at the Johns Hopkins University.

She has held teaching positions at the Gilman School, Cambridge, Massachusetts, 1899–1907, at the State Normal School in California, Pennsylvania, 1908–1909, and at Miss Madeira's School, Washington, D. C., 1910–1912. The following executive positions have been held: Head Mistress of the Charlton School, New York City, 1912–1914; Dean of Radcliffe College, 1914–1920.

The writer has travelled to the West Indies three times, to South America, to Hawaii, and she has been to Europe seven times, twice for periods of more than a year each. She is a member of Phi Beta Kappa.

CPSIA information can be obtained at www.ICGtesting.com
Printed in the USA
LVOW101606180613

339157LV00017B/789/P